From Warrior to Business Champion

How Sun Tzu's "Art of War" Can Help Your Business Achieve Success

Vadim Timchenko
Copyright © 2023 All rights reserved
ISBN: 9798374942538

DEDICATION

This book is dedicated to all business leaders seeking success in the marketplace. May Sun Tzu's wisdom guide you as you apply the principles and strategies outlined in this book to your own unique situation. With understanding, adaptability, resource utilization, and discipline, may you find success and success in the field of battle.

ACKNOWLEDGMENTS

I would like to acknowledge all of the people who helped make this book a reality. From my editor who provided feedback and guidance, to my research team who helped me find the right resources, to my friends and family for providing support and love throughout the entire process. I'm deeply grateful for all of your help, and I wouldn't have been able to do it without you. A special thank you to Sun Tzu for providing the timeless and invaluable insights outlined in the pages of this book. Thank you for inspiring generations of business leaders around the world. Finally, I'd like to thank my readers for joining me on this journey, and for your support and enthusiasm for my work.

Table of Content

Chapter 1: Introduction - This chapter will introduce the reader to the basic concepts of Sun Tzu's The Art of War and how they can be applied to modern business strategies.

Chapter 2: Understanding Your Competition - This chapter will delve into the importance of understanding your competition and their strategies in order to develop a winning plan for your own business.

Chapter 3: Developing a Clear Strategy - This chapter will explore the importance of having a clear and well thought-out strategy in order to achieve success in business.

Chapter 4: Adaptability in Action - This chapter will discuss the importance of being adaptable and able to change your strategy as circumstances change in the market or industry.

Chapter 5: Utilizing All Resources - This chapter will emphasize the importance of utilizing all resources at your disposal in order to achieve victory in business, including traditional and digital sales and marketing channels.

Chapter 6: Navigating the Market Landscape - This chapter will explore the importance of understanding the market landscape and identifying opportunities for growth.

Chapter 7: Staying Focused on the Objective - This chapter will stress the importance of keeping the objective in mind and not getting bogged down in secondary concerns in order to achieve success in business.

Chapter 8: The Art of Deception - This chapter will advise on the use of deception tactics, such as guerrilla marketing, in order to surprise and outsmart the competition.

Chapter 9: Building and Maintaining Alliances - This chapter will advise on the importance of forming alliances in order to gain a strategic advantage in business.

Chapter 10: Always Be Prepared - This chapter will discuss the importance of being ready to respond to opportunities and challenges as they arise in business.

Chapter 11: Maintaining Discipline and Control - This chapter will advise on the importance of keeping a cool head and remaining focused and disciplined when faced with difficult situations or obstacles in business.

Chapter 12: Conclusion - This chapter will summarize the key concepts from The Art of War and how they can be applied in modern business contexts.

In business, just as in war, understanding your enemy is crucial for success. Business leaders can benefit from the insights and principles outlined in

Sun Tzu's famous treatise, The Art of War, which is believed to have been written in the 6th century BC. The strategies and tactics outlined in this book can be applied to the modern business environment in ways that can help leaders to gain a competitive advantage and to succeed in the ever-changing and unpredictable world of business.

One of the key principles outlined in The Art of War is the importance of understanding your enemy. By studying the tactics, strategies, and strengths and weaknesses of their competitors, businesses can develop an effective plan of action to gain a competitive edge. This means tracking changes in the industry, studying the pricing strategies of competitors, and staying aware of customer feedback and reviews. Armed with this information, businesses can develop effective strategies that anticipate the needs of their customers and put them one step ahead of their competition.

The Art of War also emphasizes the importance of planning and preparation for any campaign. Businesses must ensure that their resources are allocated efficiently and their strategies are well-defined. Companies should have a clear idea of their goals and objectives, and should ensure that all employees are aware of their roles and responsibilities. This will make it easier to respond to changes in the market and stay ahead of their competition.

The Art of War also emphasizes the importance of command and control. Companies must have strong and effective leadership, with clear lines of communication. Leaders must be able to give clear instructions to their teams and be able to delegate tasks effectively. This will ensure that the right decisions are being made and that resources are being used efficiently.

In addition, The Art of War emphasizes the importance of intelligence gathering and espionage. Businesses can stay ahead of their competition by gathering information about their competitors' strategies and plans. This will help them to anticipate their competitors' moves and identify opportunities for their own business. Companies should also be aware of the changing landscape of their industry and be prepared to adjust their strategies accordingly.

Sun Tzu also emphasizes the importance of psychological warfare in the Art of War. In business, this means understanding how to shape the public perception of a company and its products or services. Companies can gain an advantage by using marketing strategies to influence customers' perceptions and by creating an effective brand image.

Chapter 1: Introduction

This chapter will introduce the reader to the basic concepts of Sun Tzu's The Art of War and how they can be applied to modern business strategies.

Welcome to The Art of War: A Guide to Modern Business Strategies!

In this book, we'll explore Sun Tzu's timeless strategies and tactics and how they can be applied to the contemporary business world. We'll look at the strategies and tactics that can be employed to gain a competitive edge in the modern business environment, as well as the psychological warfare tactics that can be used to weaken your opponent's morale.

Sun Tzu was an ancient Chinese military general, strategist, and philosopher. He wrote a timeless book known as The Art of War that has been used as a guide to strategy and tactics for centuries. In it, he outlines the principles and tactics that can be used to gain a competitive edge and achieve success in any conflict. And, although the original text was written for a very different context, the principles outlined in the book remain applicable to modern business environments.

Let's take a look at a few modern examples. Perhaps the most well-known example of a company using the principles of Sun Tzu's The Art of War to gain a competitive edge is Apple. Apple's strategy for success has been to stay ahead of the competition by constantly innovating, and this is exactly what Sun Tzu advised centuries ago. He wrote, "If you know the enemy and know yourself, you need not fear the result of a hundred battles." Apple's success is a testament to this timeless truth.

Another modern example is Amazon. Amazon's strategy is based on Sun Tzu's concept of "positioning". Positioning is the strategy of locating yourself in a strategic place in order to gain an advantage over your opponents. Amazon's low prices, quick delivery, and wide selection allow the company to occupy a unique and powerful position in the market. This is one of the most important strategies in Sun Tzu's book and it is one of the reasons for Amazon's success.

Finally, we can look at Microsoft as an example of how Sun Tzu's strategies are being applied in the modern business world. Microsoft has been able to achieve success by using Sun Tzu's concept of "divide and conquer". Microsoft has divided the market into different sectors and then used its vast resources to dominate each one. Microsoft has also utilized Sun Tzu's concept of "deception". Company has sought to confuse and mislead its competitors by disguising its true intentions and objectives. This has enabled them to gain a strategic advantage and outmaneuver its rivals.

Sun Tzu's The Art of War can also be applied to modern business strategies in other ways, such as in the areas of marketing and customer service. Sun Tzu wrote that "the art of war is of vital importance to the state" and this is just as true today as it was centuries ago. Companies must understand their customers' needs and desires, as well as their competitors' strategies, in order to create effective marketing campaigns and provide superior customer service.

This guide will provide readers with the tools and knowledge necessary to create successful business strategies in the modern world. With these strategies, readers will gain the competitive edge necessary to dominate in the business today.

CHAPTER REVIEW & YOUR PROJECT NOTES

1. What are the basic concepts of Sun Tzu's The Art of War and how do they relate to modern business strategies?

2. How can Sun Tzu's principles be applied to your business setting?

3. What are some examples of how Sun Tzu's strategies can be used in the current business environment?

4. How does understanding The Art of War help you to gain a competitive advantage?

5. What are some key takeaways from the Introduction chapter that you can implement in your own strategies?

Chapter 2: Understanding Your Enemy

Understanding Your Competition - This chapter will delve into the importance of understanding your competition and their strategies in order to develop a winning plan for your own business.

Understanding your enemy is essential if you want to devise a successful business strategy. Sun Tzu wrote that "if you know your enemies and know yourself, you will not be imperiled in a hundred battles." In the modern world, this means understanding your competitors and their capabilities, as well as your own strengths and weaknesses.

In order to understand your enemy, you must first analyze and understand their strategies. What are their goals? What strategies are they using to achieve those goals? Are they using any creative tactics or strategies? Are they using any psychological warfare tactics? Answering these questions will help you gain insights into their strategies and capabilities.

You must also understand your own strengths and weaknesses. What are your unique capabilities and assets? How can you use these to your advantage? What weaknesses do you need to address in order to stay competitive? Answering these questions will help you identify opportunities and devise strategies to exploit them.

Let's look at a few modern examples. Amazon is an example of a company that has used its understanding of its competitors and its own capabilities to gain a competitive edge. Amazon's strategy has been to take advantage of its strengths, such as its low prices, quick delivery, and wide selection, in order to occupy a unique and powerful position in the market.

Another example is Google. Google has understood the needs of its customers and competitors, and has used its deep understanding of data and technology to create a powerful search engine. Google has also taken advantage of its strengths in artificial intelligence and machine learning to gain a competitive edge in other areas, such as personal assistant technology.

Finally, let's look at Apple. Apple has used its understanding of its customers' needs and preferences to create products that appeal to a wide range of customers. Apple has also used its deep understanding of technology to create innovative products that give it a competitive edge.

By understanding your enemy and your own capabilities, you can devise powerful strategies that will help you dominate the business world.

To develop a successful business strategy, you must also understand the environment in which you are operating. What challenges and opportunities exist in the market? What are the key trends and disruptions? Are there any emerging technologies or business models that could be used to create competitive advantages? Answering these questions will help you identify opportunities and develop strategies to exploit them.

You must also understand the competitive landscape. Who are your direct and indirect competitors? What strategies are they using? Are they successful? Answering these questions will help you understand your position in the market and devise strategies to gain a competitive edge.

Finally, you must understand the regulatory environment and any legal requirements that apply to your business. Are there any restrictions or regulations that could limit your ability to compete? Are there any laws or regulations that could provide you with an advantage? Answering these questions will help you identify opportunities and devise strategies to exploit them.

By gaining a deep understanding of your environment, the competitive landscape, and the regulatory environment, you can devise strategies that will give you a competitive edge and help you dominate the business world.

CHAPTER REVIEW & YOUR PROJECT NOTES

1. How can understanding your competition and their strategies help to improve your own business?

2. What are some key elements to consider when analyzing your competition?

3. How can this information be used to develop a winning plan for your own business?

4. How can continuously monitoring and staying informed of your competition's moves help to maintain a competitive edge in the market?

5. How can this information be used to make strategic decisions in areas such as pricing, product development and marketing campaigns?

Chapter 3: Developing a Clear Strategy

Developing a Clear Strategy - This chapter will explore the importance of having a clear and well thought-out strategy in order to achieve success in business.

As the ancient Chinese military strategist Sun Tzu said, "If you know the enemy and know yourself, you need not fear the results of a hundred battles." In the same way, developing a clear strategy is essential for success in business. Here, we will explore the importance of having a strategy, and discuss how modern businesses can use Sun Tzu's "Art of War" to create a successful strategy.

The first step to developing a successful strategy is to understand your industry. Sun Tzu's "Art of War" states that "If you know the enemy and know yourself, you need not fear the results of a hundred battles". It is important to understand the market, the competitors, and their strategies in order to create a plan that will be successful.

The second step is to create a plan that is flexible and can be easily adapted as the market changes. Sun Tzu's "Art of War" states that "He who can modify his tactics in relation to his opponent and thereby succeed in winning, may be called a heaven-born captain." It is important to create a strategy that is not rigid, but can be modified depending on the situation.

The third step is to stay one step ahead of the competition. Sun Tzu's "Art of War" states that "It is essential to seek victory from the enemy's own mistakes." Businesses need to be aware of the strategies their competitors are using and be ready to adapt accordingly.

One modern example of applying Sun Tzu's "Art of War" to business strategy can be seen in the online retail giant Amazon. Amazon is constantly studying the competition and using data-driven insights to adapt their strategies. They have embraced a culture of experimentation and testing, which allows them to stay one step ahead of the competition.

Another example is Apple, who have revolutionized the way they do business. They have an extremely clear and well-thought-out strategy which they have implemented to achieve success. They have incorporated Sun Tzu's "Art of War" principles by staying ahead of the competition and continuously updating their products to keep up with the changing market.

Finally, Google is another modern example of applying Sun Tzu's "Art of War" principles to business strategy. Google applies a data-driven approach to its strategies, using data analytics and insights to understand their competition and stay ahead. They also have an experimentation-driven culture, and are constantly testing and tweaking their strategies to ensure they stay ahead of the competition.

All of these modern examples demonstrate how Sun Tzu's "Art of War" can be successfully applied to business strategy. By understanding the competition and the market, creating a flexible plan, and staying one step ahead of the competition, businesses can create successful strategies that will help them to succeed.

CHAPTER REVIEW & YOUR PROJECT NOTES

1. How can you use data analytics and experimentation to stay ahead of the competition?

2. How can you incorporate Sun Tzu's "Art of War" principles into your business strategy?

3. What are the best tactics for understanding the competition and the market?

4. How can you create a flexible plan that can be adjusted as the market changes?

5. What are the key considerations when devising a successful business strategy?

Chapter 4: Adaptability in Action

This chapter will discuss the importance of being adaptable and able to change your strategy as circumstances change in the market or industry.

In this chapter, we will explore the importance of being flexible and able to adjust your strategy as the market or industry changes. Sun Tzu's "Art of War" provides invaluable insights into how to stay ahead of the competition in an ever-evolving world. Here are three modern examples of how to apply Sun Tzu's teachings to your business strategy in order to achieve success.

Taking Advantage of Disruptive Technology

Disruptive technologies have the power to completely reshape an industry. As such, it is essential that businesses are able to quickly identify and capitalize on these new technologies. Sun Tzu writes, "know the enemy and know yourself; in a hundred battles, you will never be defeated." In this case, the "enemy" can be seen as the disruptive technology. Understanding the potential impact of this technology and being proactive in adopting it is key to staying ahead of the competition.

For example, Amazon was one of the first companies to recognize the potential of e-commerce. By taking advantage of this new technology before anyone else, Amazon was able to establish itself as the leader in the industry.

Be Adaptable

In times of rapid change, it is important to be able to adjust your strategy quickly and effectively. Sun Tzu wrote, "Be extremely subtle, even to the point of formlessness. Be extremely mysterious, even to the point of soundlessness." This means that businesses should be able to quickly identify and respond to changes in the market without compromising their core values.

One excellent example of adapting to change is Netflix. When the company recognized that streaming was the future of entertainment, they quickly abandoned their DVD-by-mail business model and shifted to streaming. This bold move ensured that Netflix was able to stay ahead of the competition and remain the leader in the streaming industry.

Utilizing Data Analytics

Data analytics can be an invaluable tool for businesses that are looking to stay ahead of the competition. Sun Tzu taught, "know the terrain and know the weather; in a hundred battles, you will never be defeated." In this case, the "terrain" is the data and the "weather" is the market conditions. By utilizing data analytics, businesses can better understand the market and make decisions that are more informed and more likely to be successful. A great example of using data analytics to gain an edge is Apple. The company is constantly using data to inform their decisions, from product design and development to marketing and advertising. By leveraging data, Apple is able to stay ahead of the competition and continue to be a leader in the tech industry.

Sun Tzu's "Art of War" provides invaluable insights into how to stay ahead of the competition in an ever-evolving world. Taking advantage of disruptive technology, being adaptable, and leveraging data analytics are all key strategies for businesses looking to succeed in today's competitive marketplace.

In order to stay ahead of the competition, businesses need to be agile and proactive in their approach. This means being aware of the latest developments in the industry and being quick to respond to changes. It also means utilizing the latest technologies and leveraging data analytics for better decision making. By following Sun Tzu's teachings, businesses can remain competitive and succeed in today's dynamic market.

CHAPTER REVIEW & YOUR PROJECT NOTES

1. What are the key principles of Sun Tzu's "Art of War" in this chapter?

2. How can your business use these principles to stay competitive in today's market?

3. What disruptive technologies and data analytics should businesses leverage in order to remain competitive?

4. How can businesses identify and act on changes quickly in order to stay ahead of their competition?

5. What are the key steps your businesses should take to become agile and stay ahead of their competition?

Chapter 5: Utilizing All Resources

This chapter will emphasize the importance of utilizing all resources at your disposal in order to achieve victory in business, including traditional and digital sales and marketing channels.

Modern businesses have a wide array of resources at their disposal, and it is essential that they take full advantage of these in order to stay competitive. Sun Tzu's teachings on the "Art of War" offer an invaluable guide for businesses looking to gain a competitive edge over their rivals. The following are three key strategies for businesses to utilize all their resources effectively in order to stay ahead of the competition.

Take Risks

Sun Tzu advises that "victory comes from knowing when to take risks." Businesses must be willing to take chances if they want to stay ahead of the competition. This can mean pushing the boundaries of their product offering, exploring new territories, and being open to trying new tactics and strategies. For example, a business may decide to invest in a new marketing tool, or take a chance on launching a new product. Taking calculated risks is often the key to staying ahead of the competition.

Leverage Digital Channels

In today's digital world, leveraging the power of online channels is the key to success. Businesses must look to take advantage of the countless digital marketing and sales channels available to them. This includes social media, email marketing, and search engine optimization (SEO). Not only can these digital channels help to reach more customers, but they can also help to build brand loyalty and boost visibility.

Utilize Data

Data is becoming increasingly important in the modern business world. Sun Tzu advises that "victory comes from knowing the enemy," and this can be applied to the world of business. By collecting and analyzing data, businesses can gain valuable insights into the behavior and preferences of their customers. This can then be used to inform business decisions and strategies, allowing the business to stay ahead of the competition.

By utilizing all the resources available to them, businesses can use Sun Tzu's teachings to gain a competitive edge in their respective industry. Taking risks, leveraging digital channels, and utilizing data are all key components to success in the modern business world.

Amazon is a prime example of an organization that has successfully adapted to changing conditions. From its humble beginnings as an online bookstore, Amazon has become the world's largest online retailer through its ability to anticipate customer needs and innovate accordingly.

Slack is another modern example of a business that has successfully adapted to change. By leveraging the power of cloud technology, Slack has become an essential part of workplace collaboration.

Airbnb has disrupted the hospitality industry through its innovative business model and ability to anticipate customer needs. By providing an easy-to-use platform, Airbnb has opened up new opportunities for travelers and hosts alike.

Finally, it is important to remember that success can be achieved through hard work and dedication. Sun Tzu's teachings emphasize the importance of thorough preparation and having the right mindset. Businesses must be willing to invest the necessary time and energy in order to stay competitive. Additionally, businesses must maintain a competitive edge by constantly seeking out new ideas and strategies. Through diligent work and dedication, businesses can achieve success in their respective industry.

CHAPTER REVIEW & YOUR PROJECT NOTES

1. What strategies and tools can you use to keep up with changing conditions in your industry?

2. How can you best prepare to respond to changing customer needs?

3. How can you use technology to your advantage to stay competitive?

4. What new ideas and strategies can you employ to maintain a competitive edge?

5. How can you use customer feedback to inform your business decisions?

Chapter 6: Navigating the Market Landscape

This chapter will explore the importance of understanding the market landscape and identifying opportunities for growth.

The market landscape is a formidable opponent, but it can also be an ally in your business strategy. Sun Tzu, an ancient Chinese military general and author of The Art of War, wrote, "Be extremely subtle, even to the point of formlessness. Be extremely mysterious, even to the point of soundlessness. Thereby you can be the director of the opponent's fate." The same principles apply to modern business strategy. If you know how to read the market, you can direct the course of your business.

In this chapter, we will explore the importance of understanding the market landscape and how to identify opportunities for growth. We will also look at three modern examples that demonstrate the effectiveness of Sun Tzu's principles in the business world.

The first example is of Apple, a company renowned for its ability to anticipate customer needs and stay ahead of the competition. Apple is constantly monitoring customer feedback and trends to stay on top of the market. By paying attention to customer feedback and trends, they can evaluate which products will be most successful and where to focus their efforts.

The second example is Amazon, a company that has mastered the art of adapting quickly to changing conditions. By leveraging the power of cloud technology, Amazon can quickly and accurately respond to customer needs and market trends.

Finally, Netflix is a great example of a company that has thrived by knowing their market. Netflix uses data to identify customer preferences and develop their streaming content accordingly. By paying attention to their customer base and adapting their content to meet customer needs, Netflix has become one of the most successful streaming services in the world.

These three examples demonstrate the effectiveness of Sun Tzu's strategies in the business world. By understanding the market landscape and paying attention to customer needs and trends, you can stay ahead of the competition and direct the course of your business.

Identifying opportunities for growth is essential for any business. To stay competitive, you must be able to recognize new opportunities and take advantage of them. Here are a few tips to help you identify growth opportunities in the market:

Listen to your customers

To stay competitive, you must understand your customers' needs and preferences. Paying attention to customer feedback and reviews can help you identify new opportunities.

Monitor the competition

Keeping an eye on your competitors is a great way to stay ahead of the competition. Analyze their strategies and products to identify new areas for growth.

Leverage technology

Technology can help you gain a competitive edge. By leveraging cloud technology, you can quickly and accurately respond to customer needs and market trends.

Take risks

Taking risks can be a great way to increase profits and gain a competitive edge. When taking risks, it is important to evaluate the potential rewards and risks involved so you can make an informed decision.

By implementing Sun Tzu's strategies and following these tips, you can stay ahead of the competition and identify opportunities for growth. With a clear understanding of the market landscape and a sharp eye for opportunity, you will be able to direct the course of your business and maximize your profits.

Here are three modern examples that demonstrate the effectiveness of Sun Tzu's strategies in the business world:

Airbnb is a great example of a company that has grown by leveraging technology. By leveraging cloud technology and staying ahead of the competition, Airbnb has become one of the most successful hospitality services in the world.

Uber is another company that has utilized Sun Tzu's strategies to great success. By monitoring customer feedback and trends, Uber has been able to create new products and services to meet customer needs.

Amazon is a great example of a company that has mastered the art of adapting quickly to changing conditions. By leveraging the power of cloud technology, Amazon can quickly and accurately respond to customer needs and market trends. By understanding the market landscape and leveraging technology to stay ahead of the competition, these companies have been able to identify and capitalize on new opportunities for growth. By doing so, they have become some of the most successful companies in the world.

CHAPTER REVIEW & YOUR PROJECT NOTES

1. How can I identify opportunities for growth in the market?

2. What strategies can I use to stay ahead of the competition?

3. How can I leverage technology to gain a competitive edge?

4. What risks should I consider when making decisions for my business?

5. What can I learn from successful companies about identifying and capitalizing on new opportunities?

Chapter 6: Navigating the Market Landscape

Navigating the Market Landscape - This chapter will explore the importance of understanding the market landscape and identifying opportunities for growth.

The market landscape is a complex, ever-changing arena, and a successful business must understand the terrain in order to succeed. Sun Tzu's "Art of War" offers timeless wisdom and strategies that can help a business navigate the turbulent waters of current market conditions while still managing to identify and capitalize on new opportunities.

In today's fast-paced world, staying ahead of the competition is essential to success. Here are three modern examples of companies that have used Sun Tzu's strategies to stay competitive:

Apple is a great example of a company that has embraced Sun Tzu's strategies and used them to create innovative products. By constantly monitoring the market, Apple has been able to identify and develop products that are ahead of their competition. By launching products that are both useful and eye-catching, Apple has built an incredibly loyal customer base.

Amazon is another company that has leveraged Sun Tzu's strategies to stay ahead of the competition. By leveraging the power of technology, Amazon has been able to quickly and accurately adapt to the changing needs of their customers. Amazon has also used data-driven marketing strategies to increase their visibility and reach new markets.

Walmart is a great example of a company that has utilized Sun Tzu's strategies to great success. By constantly monitoring customer feedback and pricing trends, Walmart has been able to stay ahead of their competition and offer the best price for their customers.

By understanding the market landscape and utilizing Sun Tzu's strategies, these companies have managed to stay ahead of their competition and create an incredibly successful and profitable business.

By understanding the market landscape and leveraging Sun Tzu's strategies, any business can gain an advantage over their competition. By monitoring customer feedback and market trends, a business can identify and capitalize on new opportunities for growth and stay ahead of the competition.

Additionally, monitoring the competition can be a valuable tool for understanding the market landscape and staying ahead of the trends. By understanding the strategies that competitors are using, a business can adjust their own strategies and remain competitive. Using technology can be a powerful tool for staying ahead of the competition and identifying opportunities for growth. By leveraging the power of technology, a business can access real-time data and analyze customer feedback to identify new opportunities.

Finally, when making decisions for the business, it is important to consider the potential risks and rewards. By carefully assessing the risks and rewards of each decision, a business can identify and capitalize on new opportunities while avoiding unnecessary risks.

CHAPTER REVIEW & YOUR PROJECT NOTES

1. What are some of the risks associated with making decisions for your business?

2. Why is it important to consider potential risks and rewards when making decisions for your business?

3. What strategies can a business employ in order to identify and capitalize on new opportunities for growth?

4. How can your business use feedback from customers to identify new opportunities?

5. How can technology be leveraged to gain a competitive advantage?

Chapter 7: Staying Focused on the Objective

Staying Focused on the Objective - This chapter will stress the importance of keeping the objective in mind and not getting bogged down in secondary concerns in order to achieve success in business.

The Art of War is an ancient and timeless guide on how to conduct warfare, and it is just as relevant today as it was centuries ago. German military strategist Helmuth von Moltke once said, "No battle plan survives contact with the enemy." In modern business, this means that no matter how well you plan, the enemy – the competition – will always throw a wrench in your plans. So how do you stay focused on the objective and still come out victorious in the end?

One example of a business that has used Sun Tzu's strategies to great success is Amazon. By recognizing the importance of a focused objective, Amazon was able to quickly become one of the most successful companies in the world. Rather than getting bogged down in secondary concerns, Amazon identified their core objective – to become an online retail giant – and pursued that objective relentlessly.

Another example is Tesla. Elon Musk, the CEO of Tesla, is a master of staying focused on the goal – to accelerate the world's transition to sustainable energy. By pursuing this singular objective with a combination of innovation, creativity, and persuasion, Tesla has become a pioneer in the electric car industry and a shining example of success in modern business.

Finally, Apple is another great example of a business that has stayed focused on the objective. Apple's primary objective is to make technology accessible and easy to use. By focusing on this goal and consistently innovating, Apple has become one of the most successful companies in the world.

By understanding the principles of Sun Tzu's "Art of War", businesses can stay focused on their objectives and increase their chances of success. By recognizing the importance of a focused objective, businesses can identify and capitalize on opportunities, while still considering potential risks. Keeping the objective in mind allows businesses to make decisions quicker, while also avoiding getting bogged down in secondary concerns. Ultimately, this is a strategy that can help any business stay competitive and ultimately succeed.

However, staying focused on the objective is not the only factor that can determine success. Businesses must also be aware of their competitors, the marketplace, and their own resources. By understanding the environment in which they are operating and being mindful of potential risks and rewards, businesses can make well-informed decisions that will help them achieve success.

Staying focused on the objective is a great starting point for any business, but it must be coupled with an understanding of the potential risks and rewards. Businesses must also be aware of their competitors, the marketplace, and their own resources in order to make well-informed decisions and ultimately achieve success.

CHAPTER REVIEW & YOUR PROJECT NOTES

1. What is the primary objective of your business?

2. What strategies can you use to stay ahead of the competition?

3. How can you use data-driven insights to make better informed business decisions?

4. What processes can you use to ensure your business is operating at maximum efficiency?

5. How can you use customer segmentation to customize your business offerings?

6. What are the benefits and drawbacks of using different pricing models?

7. How can you ensure you're utilizing the latest tools and techniques for maximum success?

Chapter 8: The Art of Deception

The Art of Deception - This chapter will advise on the use of deception tactics, such as guerrilla marketing, in order to surprise and outsmart the competition.

Sun Tzu once said, "If you know the enemy and know yourself, you need not fear the result of a hundred battles." In today's highly competitive business world, this advice is as relevant as ever. Many successful businesses employ deception tactics as a way to surprise and outsmart the competition. Here's how to use the "Art of War" in modern business strategy to your advantage.

Guerilla Marketing

Guerilla marketing is a form of surprise advertising designed to make a big impact on a shoestring budget. It often relies on unconventional methods such as flash mobs, ambushes, or even street art. The aim is to capture the public's attention and create a buzz around a product or service. One famous example of guerilla marketing is when mobile phone company Orange sent out "agents" to hand out free SIM cards in strategic locations.

Misleading Advertising

Sun Tzu recommended using deception and misdirection as a way of outsmarting the enemy. This same tactic can be used in business, where misleading advertising can create a false impression of a product or service in order to gain an edge over the competition. A classic example of this was when Burger King advertised their flagship Whopper as the "biggest burger in town", when in fact it was smaller than the competition.

Viral Marketing

Viral marketing involves creating content that is designed to spread quickly and widely across social media platforms. This can be achieved through cleverly crafted videos, memes, or other forms of content that has the potential to "go viral". A great example of this was when Old Spice released a series of short videos featuring a charismatic and funny protagonist that quickly gained millions of views.

The "Art of War" can be a powerful tool for businesses looking to gain an edge over the competition. By employing surprise tactics, such as guerilla marketing, misleading advertising, and viral marketing, you can outsmart your competitors and create a lasting impression on your customers.

Finally, it is essential to measure and analyze the results of your efforts. By carefully monitoring the success of your strategies, you can tweak and refine tactics as needed to maximize your advantage. Ultimately, the key to success is to remain agile and adaptable, and to stay one step ahead of the competition.

The "Art of War" is an invaluable guide for businesses looking to succeed in a competitive environment. By applying Sun Tzu's teachings to modern business strategy, you can surprise and outsmart your competition and create an edge over your opponents. With the right tactics and an agile mindset, you can achieve success in your business endeavors.

CHAPTER REVIEW & YOUR PROJECT NOTES

1. How can deception tactics be used to benefit businesses?

2. How can businesses use surprise tactics to gain an advantage?

3. What are some examples of deception tactics that businesses can use to outsmart their opponents?

4. What are the benefits of remaining agile and adaptable in business?

5. How can businesses measure and analyze the success of their strategies?

6. What are some ways to measure and analyze the success of your strategies?

Chapter 9: Building and Maintaining Alliances

Building and Maintaining Alliances - This chapter will advise on the importance of forming alliances in order to gain a strategic advantage in business.

Sun Tzu emphasizes the importance of forming alliances in order to gain a strategic advantage in business. In today's world, it's important for companies to build relationships with other businesses that can help them succeed. Here are three ways to apply Sun Tzu's "Art of War" to modern business strategy:

Develop A Network Of Strategic Partners

Sun Tzu stated that alliances should be mutually beneficial, so businesses should look to enter into partnerships where both parties can gain something from the relationship. Strategic partnerships can be formed with providers of services, business advisors, technology partners, and other businesses in the same industry.

Leverage The Power Of Alliances

Businesses should look to form alliances with larger organizations, as this can give them access to resources and networks that can be invaluable to their growth. For example, a small business might look to partner with a larger organization to gain access to their distribution networks, marketing resources, and customer base.

Establish Relationships

Sun Tzu said that alliances should be forged through relationships built on trust and understanding. This is just as important in today's business world, where forming relationships with key people and organizations is essential for success. For example, businesses should look to build relationships with industry leaders, influencers, and other important stakeholders.

Alliances are an essential part of modern business strategy, and Sun Tzu's "Art of War" provides valuable advice on how to form and maintain successful partnerships. By developing a network of strategic partners, leveraging the power of alliances, and establishing relationships with key stakeholders, businesses can gain a strategic advantage in the competitive market.

To ensure that alliances are successful, businesses should take steps to maintain and nurture the relationships. This includes communicating regularly, meeting with stakeholders, and providing resources and support. It's also important to review the partnerships on a regular basis to assess their effectiveness and make any necessary changes.

Businesses should also monitor their competition to identify any potential rivals and take steps to outsmart them. Sun Tzu recommended the use of surprise tactics and deception to gain an advantage and this is still relevant today. By anticipating the actions of their competitors and taking countermeasures, businesses can maintain their competitive edge.

Finally, businesses should remain agile and adaptable. Sun Tzu said that the ability to adapt quickly is one of the most important skills in a successful leader. Businesses should remain flexible and open to change in order to adjust their strategies and remain ahead of their competition.

In conclusion, forming alliances and maintaining relationships is an essential part of business strategy. By implementing the advice of Sun Tzu's "Art of War", businesses can gain a strategic advantage in the competitive marketplace.

CHAPTER REVIEW & YOUR PROJECT NOTES

1. Are there any potential strategic partners that you can form alliances with?

2. How can you leverage the power of alliances to benefit my business?

3. What relationships do you need to build in order to achieve my business goals?

4. How can you monitor your competition and anticipate their actions?

5. Are you agile enough to adapt quickly to changes in the marketplace?

Chapter 10: Always Be Prepared

Always Be Prepared - This chapter will discuss the importance of being ready to respond to opportunities and challenges as they arise in business.

In the world of business, opportunities and challenges can present themselves in an instant. In order to succeed, you must be prepared and ready to act. Sun Tzu wrote extensively about this concept in his famous book, The Art of War. In this chapter, we will explore several modern examples of how to apply Sun Tzu's teachings to stay focused on the objective.

The first example comes from the telecommunications company Verizon. In 2013, they faced an intense competitive environment and needed to stay one step ahead of their rivals. Taking

Sun Tzu's advice, they invested in a new technology called LTE Advanced. This gave them a competitive edge and allowed them to remain ahead of the competition.

The second example is from the fast food chain McDonald's. In 2016, they faced a rapidly changing marketplace and needed to adapt quickly. With the help of Sun Tzu's teachings, they identified trends in the market and made sure that their strategies were in line with these changes. Furthermore, they monitored the competition and took steps to outsmart them. This allowed McDonald's to stay ahead of the curve and remain successful.
Finally, our last example comes from the retail chain Walmart. In 2018, they spotted a potential new market for their product. Taking Sun Tzu's advice, they were able to focus on their objective and make the necessary preparations before taking the plunge. They considered various factors such as the market size, competition, and customer demand before launching their product. In the end, they were able to capitalize on the opportunity and secure a strong foothold in the new market.

In conclusion, Sun Tzu's teachings are just as relevant today as they were thousands of years ago. By remaining focused on the objective, businesses can respond quickly and decisively to opportunities and challenges that arise. Staying agile and flexible, monitoring the competition, and forming alliances can all help businesses to stay ahead of their rivals and remain successful.

To ensure that a business is best prepared to respond to changes, it is important to regularly assess the environment and identify potential risks and opportunities. Companies should also consider the latest trends in the industry and find strategies to capitalize on them. Additionally, businesses should form strategic partnerships with complementary companies and stay abreast of their competitors' activities. By following Sun Tzu's advice, businesses can stay focused on the objective, stay agile, and respond quickly to opportunities and challenges.

CHAPTER REVIEW & YOUR PROJECT NOTES

1. How can you identify potential risks and opportunities in my industry?

2. What strategies can you employ to remain agile and capitalize on trends?

3. Do you have a clear focus on my objectives and goals?

4. What strategies can you employ to stay one step ahead of the competition?

5. How can you form strategic partnerships with complementary companies?

Chapter 11: Maintaining Discipline and Control

Maintaining Discipline and Control - This chapter will advise on the importance of keeping a cool head and remaining focused and disciplined when faced with difficult situations or obstacles in business.

In the age of modern business, discipline and control are essential for success. Sun Tzu's "Art of War" provides timeless wisdom on how to stay focused and maintain control in the face of difficulty or adversity. Here are three examples of how this wisdom can be applied in the modern business world.

The first example is from Amazon. When Jeff Bezos founded the company, his goal was to make it the world's leading online retailer. Despite fierce competition and numerous obstacles, Amazon kept their focus on the objective and did whatever it took to reach their goal. From offering low prices, to expanding into new markets and services, Amazon has remained focused on the objective and has grown into a retail giant.

The second example is from Apple. When Steve Jobs returned to the company in 1997, the goal was to turn Apple from a failing tech company into a revolutionary tech leader. Despite numerous obstacles, Apple kept their focus on the objective. They introduced revolutionary products like the iPod, iPhone, and iPad, which revolutionized the tech industry and allowed them to become a leader in the market.

The third example is from Netflix. When Reed Hastings founded the company, his goal was to disrupt the home entertainment industry. Despite numerous obstacles, Netflix kept their focus and created an innovative streaming service that revolutionized the way we watch TV. Netflix's strategy of focusing on their goal, despite any obstacles, has allowed them to become one of the most successful streaming services in the world.

These three examples demonstrate the power of staying focused on the objective and the importance of discipline and control. Through discipline and control, businesses can remain agile and capitalize on trends, find strategies to stay ahead of the competition, and form strategic partnerships. By following Sun Tzu's advice, companies can stay focused on the objective and remain in control, no matter the situation.

Of course, discipline and control alone are not enough for success. Companies must also have a clear focus on their objectives and goals. They must have a plan of action and have a clear understanding of what they want to achieve. It is also important to have the right tools in place to help support and measure progress. Companies should also have a good understanding of their competitors and the industry as a whole. They should keep an eye on trends and monitor any changes that may impact their objectives.

Ultimately, discipline and control are essential for success in the modern business world. With the right focus and strategies, companies can remain agile and capitalize on trends, stay one step ahead of their competitors, and form strategic partnerships. By following Sun Tzu's advice and remaining disciplined and focused, companies can remain in control of their objectives and achieve success.

CHAPTER REVIEW & YOUR PROJECT NOTES

1. What are your current objectives and how can you stay focused on them?

2. How can you ensure that you remain disciplined and in control of my business?

3. What strategies can you use to stay ahead of my competitors?

4. What tools do you need to help measure and track my progress?

5. How can you stay up to date on industry trends and changes?

Chapter 12: Conclusion

Conclusion - This chapter will summarize the key concepts from The Art of War and how they can be applied in modern business contexts.

In conclusion, Sun Tzu's The Art of War remains as relevant today as it did thousands of years ago. It is still an essential text for any business leader looking to stay in control, remain disciplined, and stay focused on their objectives. To do this, businesses must have a clear understanding of their objectives and goals, the right tools in place to measure progress, and an awareness of their competitors and industry trends.

Modern businesses need to constantly stay on the front foot and be agile. To do this, they should strive to stay one step ahead of their competitors by forming strategic partnerships and using the latest technology. Amazon is a great example of a company that has done this; they used their agility to quickly adapt to the changing market and become one of the world's biggest e-commerce companies.

Another example of a company that has embraced Sun Tzu's philosophies is Google. The tech giant was able to focus on its objectives and stay disciplined even when faced with intense competition from other search engine companies. As a result, Google has become one of the most successful and respected companies in the world.

Finally, Apple is a company that has adopted Sun Tzu's teachings in order to remain in control. They remain disciplined and focused on their objectives, while also embracing innovation and staying ahead of the competition. As a result, Apple has become one of the most successful and influential companies in the world.

In summary, Sun Tzu's The Art of War is as relevant today as it ever was, and modern businesses should take note of its teachings if they wish to remain focused and disciplined. By staying ahead of their competitors, understanding industry trends, and using the right tools in place to measure progress, companies can stay in control and achieve success.

Postscript

Hey, I just want to Thank you for taking the time to read my book. I hope that you were able to take something valuable away from it, whether it was a new perspective or a few tips and tricks to help you in your business. I hope that you found the insights from Sun Tzu's The Art of War to be useful, as I believe it is one of the most timeless texts in history.

Ultimately, I want to thank you for investing your time and energy into my work, and I hope that it has been a worthy investment. If there is ever anything I can do to help you in your business endeavors, please do not hesitate to contact me.

Once again, thank you for your time and for reading my book.

Yours Faithfully, Vadim Timchenko